NEXT STATION 3

CLIL BOOK

Ana Elisa Martins

macmillan education

CONTENTS

		SUBJECT	THEME	LANGUAGE	MY LEARNING GOALS
UNIT 1	TRADE ROUTES PAGES 4-9	History	Movements of People, Products, and Culture	• places of production (corn field, jeans factory) • places of commerce (clothes store, food market) • trade routes (roads, rivers, ocean, air) • route types (combined land and waterway routes, land routes, maritime routes) • trade products (cinnamon, ginger, incense, silk, pepper) • modern routes (railway routes, road networks, river and maritime routes, air transport) • They go by (train). / It was on the (Silk Road).	Identify and describe the importance of trade routes
UNIT 2	HOW DO PRODUCTS GET TO YOU? PAGES 10-15	Geography	The World of Work	• food (bananas, apples, grapes, pineapples, oranges, pears, egg, strawberries, cereal, bread, butter) • processed food, whole food • sectors of the economy: primary sector (farming, mining, fishing), secondary sector (food production, clothing and textiles, electronics), tertiary sector (retail, transport, education) • There are different types of manufacturing industries. / Natural materials are transformed into products.	Describe the production and retail processes of different products
UNIT 3	MIGRATION PAGES 16-21	History	Historical Migration Issues	• countries and nationalities (the UK / British, the USA / American, Turkey / Turkish, Malaysia / Malaysian, Spain / Spanish, South Korea / South Korean) • migration (permanent, temporary, forced, voluntary, internal, international, emigrant, immigrant, migrant) • migration in history (Age of Sail, Industrial Revolution, refugee crises) • Where did the immigrants come from? / When did they emigrate? / Why did they leave their country? / What habits did they bring?	Analyze changes provoked by migration
UNIT 4	WHAT DO YOU PLAY? PAGES 22-27	PE	Sports	• sports (baseball, ice hockey, ping pong, soccer, tennis, basketball) • games (skills, friendship, entertainment) • It is competitive. / It requires physical effort. / It can be played professionally. / The rules are predefined.	Differentiate games from sports
UNIT 5	IS IT HOT OR COLD? PAGES 28-33	Math	Quantities and Measurements	• weather (sunny, snowy, cloudy, rainy, hot, cold) • temperature measurement (thermometer, Celsius and Fahrenheit scales) • days of the week (Sunday, Monday, Tuesday, Wednesday, Thursday, Friday, Saturday) • It's (sunny). • The hottest month in Ocho Rios is … / The coldest months in Ocho Rios are …	Recognize temperature as a way of measuring how hot or cold a region is
UNIT 6	CITIES PAGES 34-39	History	Transitions and Constants in Human Journeys	• places in town (library, museum, supermarket, movie theater, hospital, airport, café) • urbanization (social and cultural integration, economic development, unemployment, pollution, housing) • sustainable alternatives (vertical gardens, electric buses, solar panels, recycling, urban farming) • agriculture, economy, population, transportation, political power, BCE • The first cities were founded by… / 68% of the world population will live in cities.	Identify the changes that occurred in cities

	SUBJECT	THEME	LANGUAGE	MY LEARNING GOALS
UNIT 7 — RURAL AND URBAN WORK — PAGES 40-45	Geography	World of Work	• jobs in urban and rural areas (truck driver, nurse, vet, fisherwoman, clerk, farmer, factory worker, firefighter) • work in the country (mechanization, agriculture, monoculture, subsistence farm, polyculture, pesticides, fertilizers) and in the city (industries, businesses, factories, health care, electricity, infrastructure) • food industry (fishing, manufacturing, transporting, retail) • Most jobs in the country are related to agriculture. / Most industries and businesses are located in cities.	Compare the characteristics of work in the country and in the city
UNIT 8 — CALENDARS — PAGES 46-51	Science	Earth and the Universe	• months (January, February, March, April, May, June, July, August, September, October, November, December) • astronomical cycles (day, month, year, revolution, rotation) • calendars (Gregorian, Chinese, Hebrew, Hindu, Aztec) • Months have .... days. / The Earth takes a day to … and a year to … / The moon revolves around the Earth in …	Associate the movements of the Earth and moon with different calendars
UNIT 9 — LET'S CELEBRATE! — PAGES 52-57	Art	Integrated Arts	• special events (barbecue, birthday party, parade, picnic, wedding) • traditional celebrations (Albuquerque International Balloon Fiesta, Yi Peng Lantern Festival, La Tomatina, Carnival, Harbin Festival) • We can see or be part of many forms of artistic expression. / We can play the spoons… / We can cover our whole body in bright colors …	Value cultural differences and traditions
UNIT 10 — MATTER AND CHANGES — PAGES 58-63	Science	Matter and Energy	• materials (fabric, plastic, wood, glass) • matter (mass, volume, particles, atoms) • states of matter (solid, liquid, gas) • physical and chemical changes (melting, breaking, fermentation, boiling, burning) • Matter occupies space. / Matter can move from one state to another. / Most chemical changes cannot be reversed.	Understand how matter changes when exposed to different conditions

· ICONS ·

 **ZOOM IN**
Activities to interpret the picture of the unit opener pages

 **LISTEN**
Audio tracks to practice listening skills

 THINK    BE    LEARN    ACT    COLLABORATE / COMMUNICATE

TRADE ROUTES

UNIT 1

HISTORY

This is the port of Veracruz, in Mexico. Ports are an important economic center in coastal areas.

Is there an important port in your country?

ZOOM IN
Look at the picture.
What means of transportation do you see?

UNIT 1 — HISTORY

1 Match and answer.

Places of production

corn field

jeans factory

Places of commerce

clothes store

food market

How do these products get there?

TRACK 1

2 Listen, read, and number.

Trade Routes

Trade routes are pathways used to transport products from places of production to places of commerce. **Roads** (1), **rivers** (2), **ocean** (3), and **air** (4) are the different modes by which products can travel.

TRACK 2

3 Listen, read, and complete.

Famous Routes in History

Combined land and waterway routes

Some routes combine transportation by land and water. A very famous example is the **Incense Route**, which linked the Mediterranean World to Africa, Arabia, and India. This route was a channel for trading mainly spices and incense.

Land routes

These routes are mostly on land. The **Silk Road** joined the Eastern and Western worlds, with the trade of silk and other products.

Maritime routes

These are mainly by sea. The **Spice Route** got its name from the transportation of spices (cinnamon, pepper, ginger) from Asia and Northern Africa to Europe.

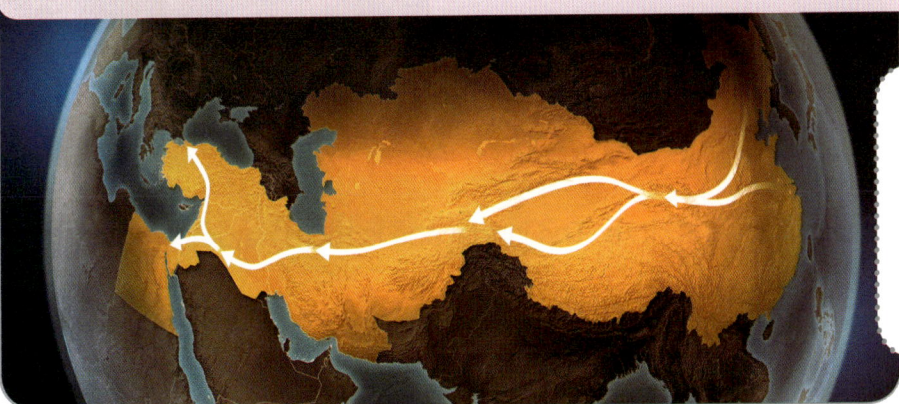

This map shows a _____ route. This is one of the routes of the _____ Road.

GLOSSARY

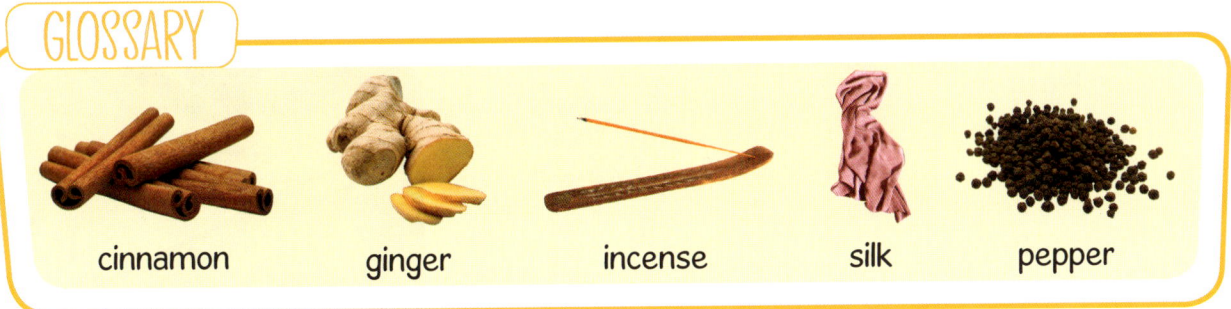

cinnamon   ginger   incense   silk   pepper

4 Read the text again and answer.

1 Which products were transported using these routes?

2 Why were these products transported from one place to another?

TRACK 3

5 Listen, read, and match.

Routes and Cities

When trade routes are very busy, cities that are on these routes can grow bigger and new cities can be created. Commerce in these areas also increases and cultural exchanges happen. For example, people learn different languages and assimilate customs from distant regions.

Important places on a trade route tend to have a **bigger population**. Places that are isolated tend to have very **small populations**.

The environment around a major route changes, too. The landscape around cities with intense commerce is less natural and more man-made. Outside trade routes, the environment tends to be more natural as there is less impact from human activity.

Gjogv, Faroe Islands, Denmark.

Istanbul, Turkey.

a It is a city of 15 million inhabitants.   (2)   **d** It was on the Silk Road.   ( )

b It is a village of 49 inhabitants.   ( )   **e** The landscape is more natural.   ( )

c It connects to only one road.   ( )   **f** The landscape is more man-made.   ( )

TRACK 4

6 Listen, read, and answer.

Modern Routes

Nowadays, **railway routes**, **road networks**, **river and maritime routes** and **air transport** are the ways to transport people and products from one place to another.

This is how we have access to products made in other places. And this is part of a process called **globalization**. Globalization is the integration and interaction among people around the world.

China's road network.

1 What is globalization?

2 Give three examples of the effects of globalization on your life.

7 Do research. Choose one of the options. Then complete the chart with your notes.

1 Amber road
2 Pre-Colombian route
3 Salt route
4 Tea route
5 Trans-Saharan trade route

name	
time	
type of route	
cities on the route	
products	
curiosities	

8 Interview a classmate that chose another route. Then swap roles.

What do you like the most about your classmate's route?

UNIT 2: HOW DO PRODUCTS GET TO YOU?

GEOGRAPHY

This is a picture of a family buying fruit at a supermarket.

Do you know where the fruit comes from?

ZOOM IN

Look at the picture.
Are these products natural or manufactured? Why?

UNIT 2

1 Label the food using the words from the box.

> bananas   apples   grapes   pineapples   oranges   pears
> egg   strawberries   cereal   bread   butter

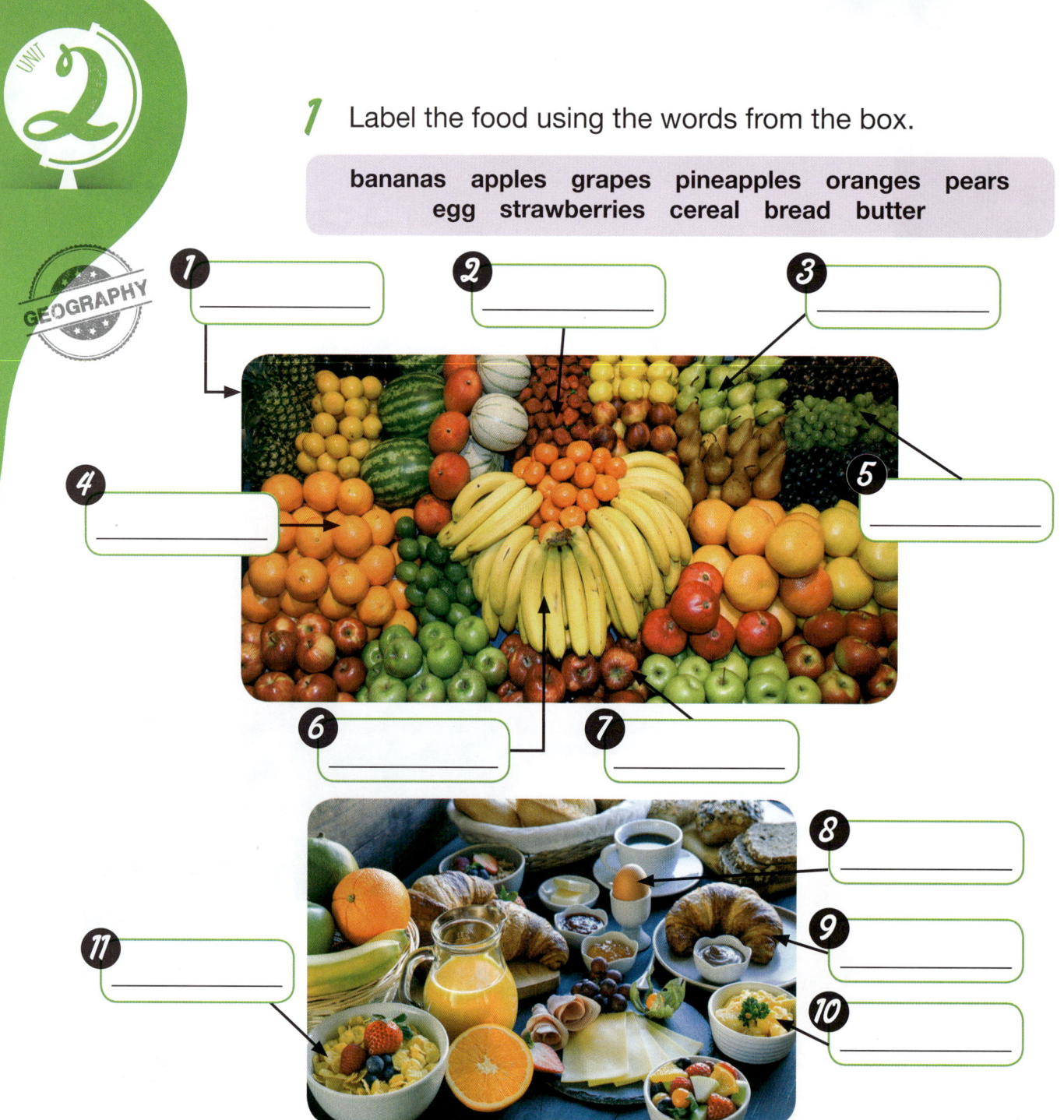

2 Look at the glossary and name the food in Activity 1 that is processed.

GLOSSARY

Processed food is food that has been cooked, canned, frozen, packaged, or changed nutritionally.
Whole food is a natural food that has little or no processing.

TRACK 5

3 Listen and read.

Economic Activities

We consume different types of products every day. These products come from different sectors of the economy: **the primary**, **the secondary**, and the **tertiary sector**.

Primary sector

Farming, **mining**, and **fishing** are activities from the primary sector. They obtain natural materials from the land and the sea.

Arable farming is the planting of crops like fruits, vegetables, grains, and seeds. Livestock farming is the activity of raising animals. The animals produce meat, eggs, milk, and wool.

Mining is the activity of taking natural materials from the Earth, like rocks and minerals.

Fishing is the activity of catching fish and other animals from rivers, lakes, and oceans.

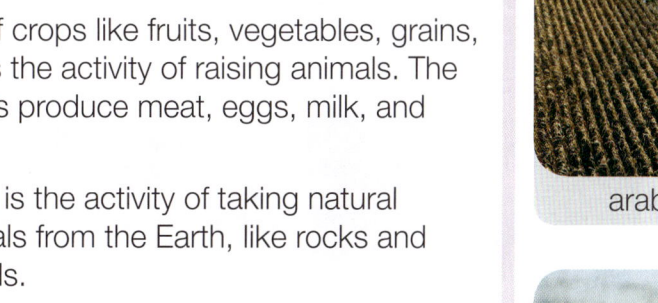
arable farming

livestock farming

mining

fishing

It's a fact!
Natural materials are processed to make other products.

gold → jewelry
fruits → jam

Think Twice

1 Give one or two examples of natural materials that are processed to make other products.

2 What natural products can be consumed without being processed?

4 Find and write.

1 What are some of the activities of the primary sector?

2 Which activity takes rocks and minerals from the Earth?

13

TRACK 6

5 Listen and read.

Secondary sector

The secondary sector is the **industrial production**. In this sector, the natural materials are transformed into products. The products are manufactured in large quantities in factories using machines.

There are different types of manufacturing industries, for example, **food production**, **clothing and textiles**, and **electronics**.

textile industry

electronic industry

food industry

Tertiary sector

The tertiary sector provides services in different areas, for example, **retail**, **education**, **transport**, etc.

retail

transport

education

6 Read the text again and answer.

1 What happens to natural materials in the secondary sector?

2 What helps the manufacturing industry produce in large quantities?

7 Look at the diagram below showing the integration of the sectors of the economy.

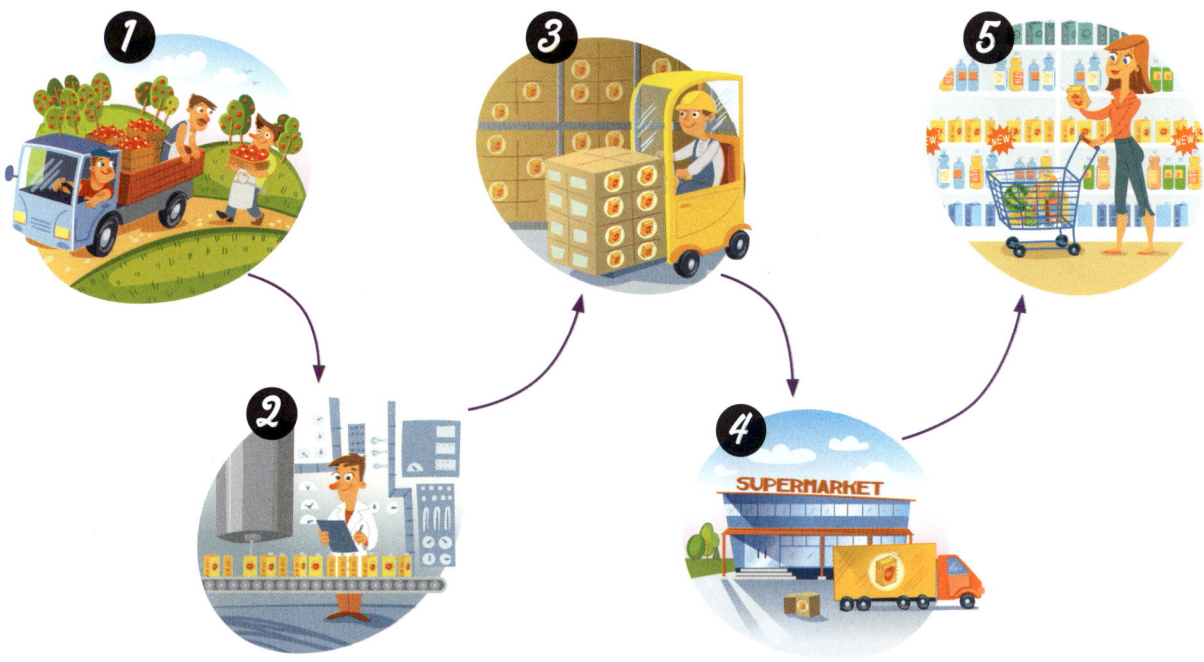

 **8** Look at the diagram again and number the sectors according to its stages.

Primary sector	Secondary sector	Tertiary sector
_____	_____	_____

 9 Research about an economic activity that is important in the region you live. Present it to your classmates.

15

MIGRATION

UNIT 3

These people are at an international airport. They are waiting for Syrians who left their country to live in Canada.

Why do people move?
Do you know anyone who left their place of birth to live in another country or city? Where do they come from?

Look at the picture.
How are these Syrians probably arriving in Canada?

UNIT 3

HISTORY

1 Look at the flags. Then read and write the name of the corresponding countries.

1. ____Turkey____ received lots of people looking for protection or asylum in 2015.

2. The _____ received hundreds of people from the Caribbean, in 1948.

3. The _____ received people from all over the world. Before 1880, most people were from Europe.

4. _____ sent workers to Germany, the USA, and the Middle East for many years.

5. _____ is the country with the third-largest population of Indians in the world.

6. _____ experienced different migratory movements in the 20th century.

2 Look at Activity 1. Match the countries and their nationalities.

Turkish — 1   American — ◯   Malaysian — ◯

Spanish — ◯   South Korean — ◯   British — ◯

TRACK 7

  3 Listen and read.

Human Migration

Migration is the situation in which people move places to look for jobs or better living conditions. Migration can be **permanent** or **temporary**, and it may be **forced** or **voluntary**.

There are two different types of human migration: **internal** and **international**.

Internal migration is the movement of people from one area to another inside a country. For example, when people move from the countryside to the city.

International migration is the movement from one country to another.

A person who leaves their country to settle in a new one is called an **emigrant**. In the new country, this same person is called an **immigrant**. Immigrants and emigrants are both considered **migrants**.

It's a fact!
Work is the main reason why people migrate internationally.

European immigrants at Ellis Island, USA, in 1921.

Italians emigrants leaving their homeland.

4 Read the text again and answer.

1 What is migration?
2 There are two types of migration: internal and international. What is the difference between them?
3 Who are migrants?

Think Twice

1 Do you think human migration is a recent movement? Why? Why not?

2 What problems can an immigrant face when arriving at a new country?

UNIT 3 — HISTORY

TRACK 8

5 Listen and read. Then match.

Migrations in History

Migration is not a new thing. Throughout history, humankind has faced different large migration flows.

1. In the 16th century, during the period known as the **Age of Sail**, explorers discovered new lands and routes around the world. Many people migrated to these new lands at that time, motivated by better living conditions. But others were captured and transported as slaves from Africa to European colonies.

2. In the 18th century, the **Industrial Revolution** improved transportation and contributed to a new mass migration. Over 50 million people left Europe for North America. Many of them to escape poverty and work in factories in the New World.

3. Large migrations also happened in more recent years. The **refugee crisis**, which started in the 21st century, is an example. Civil war forced many people to leave countries like Syria. At the end of 2015, there were 21 million refugees worldwide. Europe was the main destination of those people.

Workers in a factory.

Refugees arriving in Europe.

Portuguese and the Great Navigations.

6 Read the text again. Then complete the timeline.

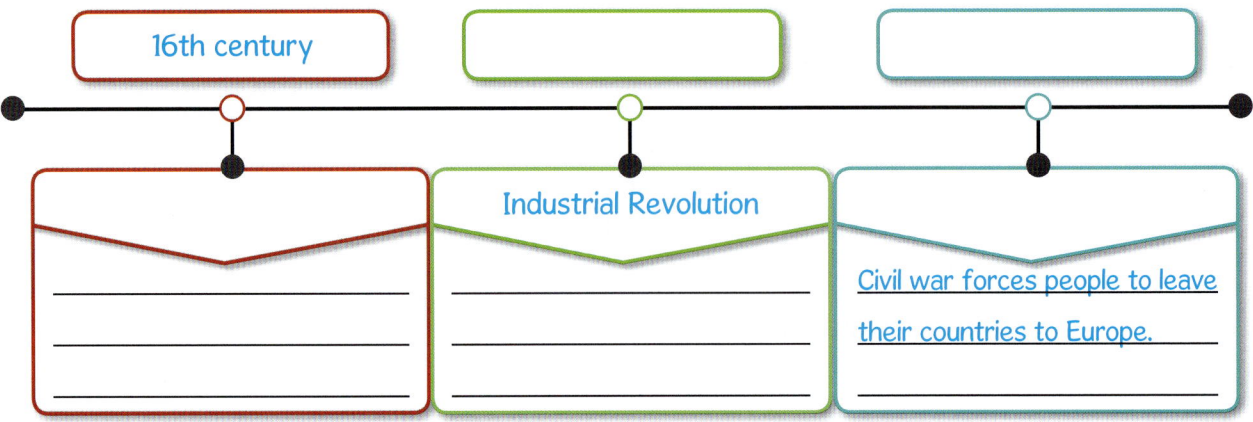

16th century

Industrial Revolution

Civil war forces people to leave their countries to Europe.

20

TRACK 9

7 Listen and read. Then number.

Immigration can have many impacts on a country's population. It can influence people, adding or changing elements in their culture, such as **food** (**1**), **habits** (**2**), and **music** (**3**).

Eating at the table.

Pizza, an Italian food.

Samba, a Brazilian music style with African roots.

8 Research about immigrants who came to your country. Complete the chart and present.

Where did the immigrants come from?	
When did they emigrate?	
Why did they leave their country?	
What habits did they bring?	

WHAT DO YOU PLAY?

UNIT 4

These three kids are in the UK. They're playing a game.

Which sport is this?
Can you name some popular sports in your country?

Look at the picture.
Is it an official competition? Why / Why not?

UNIT 4

1 Look at the pictures and complete.

1
B _A_ S _E_ B _A_ LL

2
___ C ___ H ___ C K ___ Y

3
P ___ NG P ___ NG

4
S ___ C C ___ R

5
T ___ N N ___ S

6
B ___ S K ___ T B ___ L L

2 Complete the sentences with the names of the sports mentioned in Activity 1.

1 ___Baseball___ and _____ are popular sports in the United States.

2 _____ is the official national winter sport of Canada.

3 China is the most successful country in olympic _____.

4 _____ is a racket sport that is very popular in Australia.

5 The FIFA World Cup is a _____ competition that takes place every four years.

TRACK 10

3 Listen and read.

Sports vs Games

Do you know the difference between *game* and *sport*? We often confuse these two words, but they have different meanings.

Sports are competitive activities that require physical effort, knowledge, and skill. They are defined by rules that guarantee a fair competition. A person who practices a sport following all these rules is called an athlete.

Games are activities that also involve skill, knowledge, or physical effort. But in games the players can create or adapt the rules. People usually play games with a sense of friendship, but games can also be competitive.

The Olympic Games are played to strengthen the relationships between countries. Despite the name, the Olympic Games is actually a sports event!

Sports have strict rules that athletes and teams need to follow.

Games are played with a sense of friendship and entertainment.

It's a fact!
Sports have the biggest television audiences. The most popular are the Summer Olympics and the FIFA World Cup.

Think Twice

1 What is the main difference between a sport and a game?
2 Do you practice any sports? What games do you like to play?

4 Check (✓) the information according to the text.

	game	sport
It is competitive.		
It requires physical effort.		
It can be played professionally.		
The players create the rules.		
The rules are predefined.		

TRACK 11

5 Listen and read. Then write *game* or *sport* under each picture.

> Sports are played professionally, but most sports can be played as games in informal situations, outside of official competitions. For example, when you play tennis with a friend in a court without a net.
>
> At school, we usually learn the rules of a sport and try to follow them. But we often play it for educational or recreational purposes and don't need to follow the rules strictly.
>
> Most sports originated as games and only later organized rules and standards to become an official sport. Basketball, for example, was played with a soccer-style ball and players threw the ball at peach baskets.

ice hockey | baseball

1 _____ 2 _____

3 _____ 4 _____

soccer

5 _____ 6 _____

6 Go back to the unit opener pages and answer.

Is basketball being played as a sport or a game in the picture? Why?

_____
_____

26

7 In groups, research or create a game based on a sport. Follow the steps below.

1. Choose an existing sport you are familiar with.
2. Research its history before it was an official sport **or** create or adapt its rules as a game.
3. Write about it in the lines below.

_____
_____
_____
_____
_____
_____
_____
_____
_____

4. Look for objects that can be used to play it. For example: a ruler can be a bat or a racket, your desk can be a goal, a sheet of paper can be a ball.

5. Explain it to the class as a group and demonstrate it. Watch out for your teacher and colleagues' safety and mind the materials!
6. Clean up after yourselves.

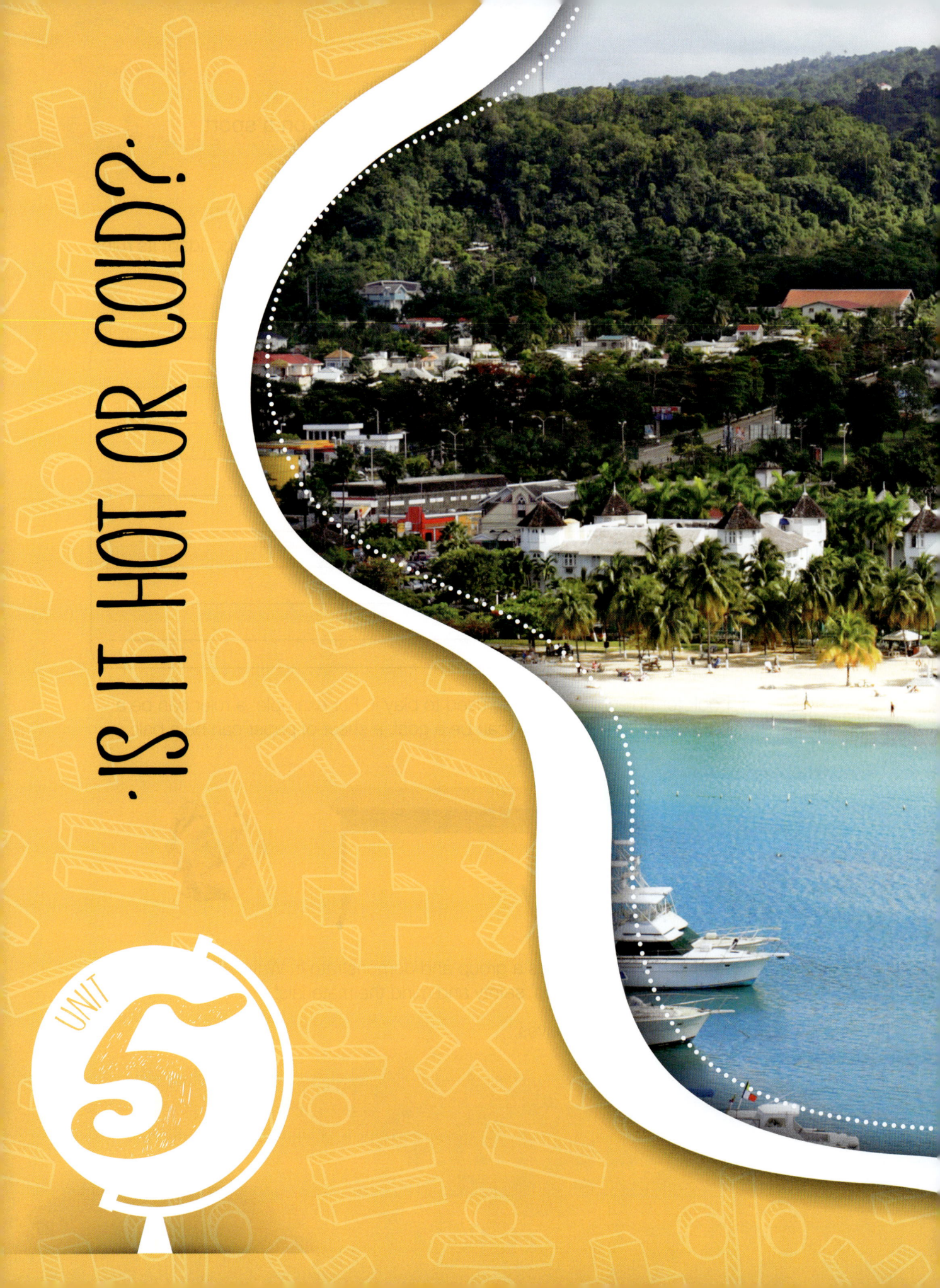

IS IT HOT OR COLD?

UNIT 5

UNIT 5

MATH

1 Look at the icons and write the name of the weather.

1

____

2

____

3

____

4

____

5

____

6

____

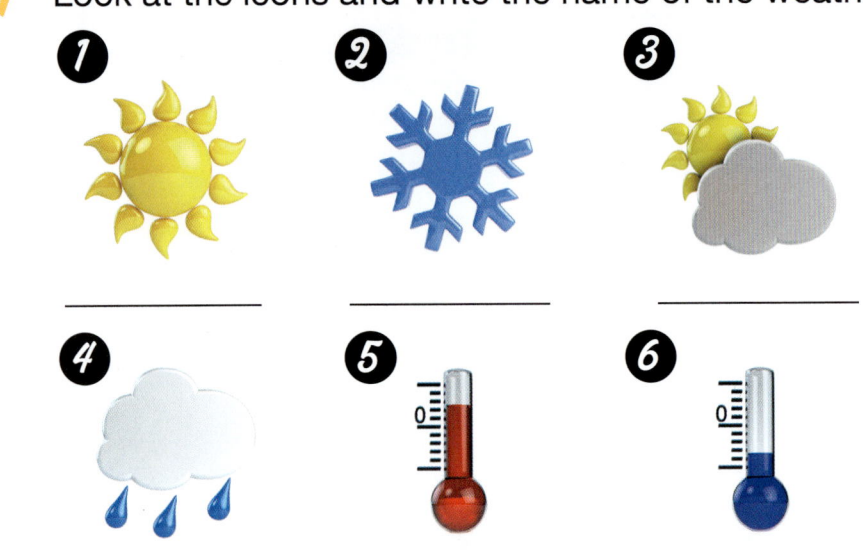

2 Complete the bingo card with pictures of weather icons. Play the game in groups.

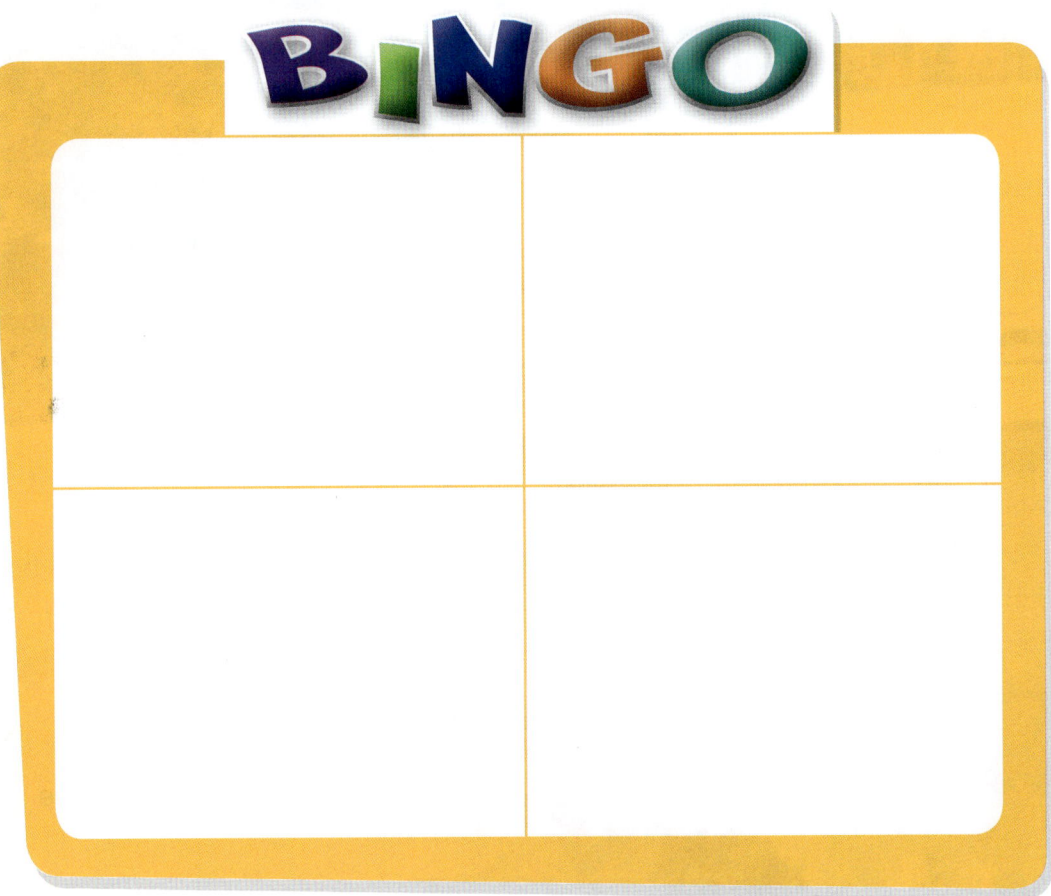

TRACK 12

3 Listen and read.

Measuring Temperatures

Temperature is the amount of heat measured in a place. We can measure the temperature of air, liquids, or objects using a **thermometer**.

The two commonly used scales to measure temperature are **Celsius** (°C) and **Fahrenheit** (°F). The United States use the Fahrenheit scale, but Celsius is the most used one around the world. Each scale gives a different number for a measure of temperature.

Celsius thermometer   Fahrenheit thermometer

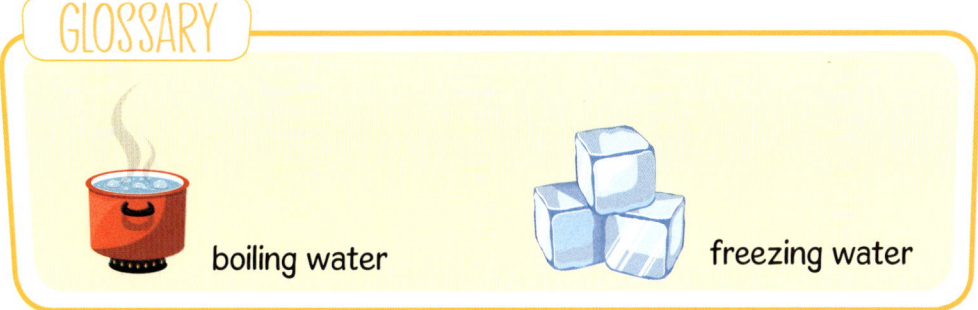

4 Find and answer.

1 How can we measure the temperature?

_____.

2 What is the temperature of boiling water in Fahrenheit?

_____.

Think Twice

1 What is the temperature scale used in your country?

2 What is another way to measure the weather temperature without using a thermometer?

31

UNIT 5

MATH

5 Look at the bar graphs below. They show the maximum and minimum temperatures in Ocho Rios, Jamaica.

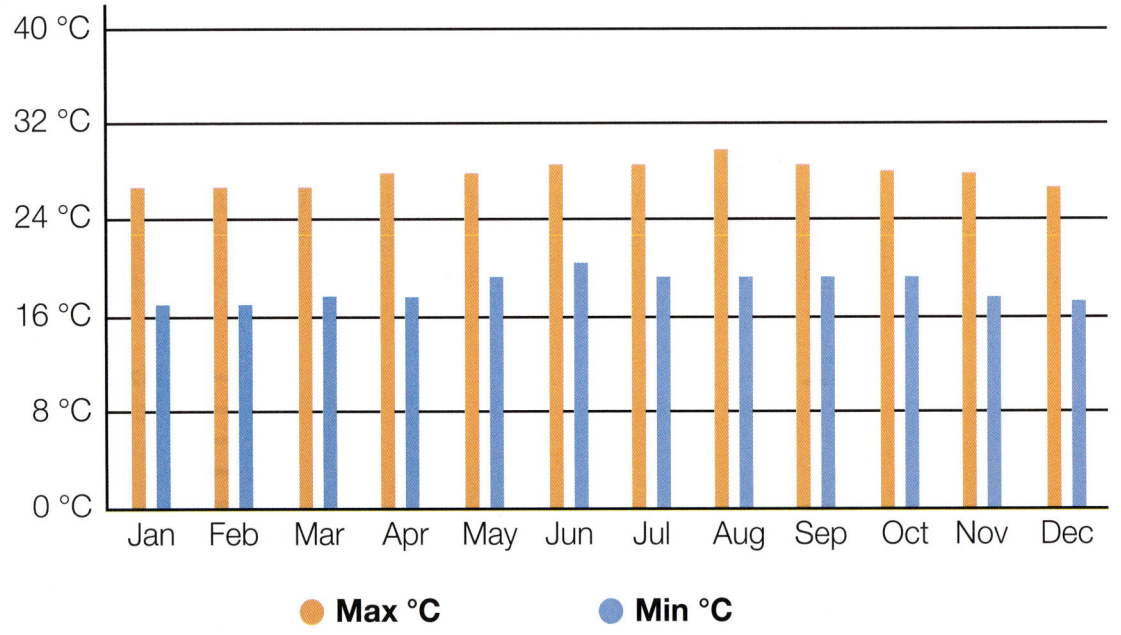

	Jan	Feb	Mar	Apr	May	Jun	Jul	Aug	Sep	Oct	Nov	Dec
Min °C	17	17	19	19	20	21	20	20	20	20	19	18
Max °C	27	27	27	28	28	29	29	30	29	28	28	27

Based on: <https://www.weather2visit.com/central-america/jamaica/ocho-rios.htm >. Accessed on: May 16, 2019.

GLOSSARY

Max = Maximum

Min = Minimum

6 Complete the panel with the maximum and minimum temperatures according to the graphs.

↑ ______ °C

↓ ______ °C

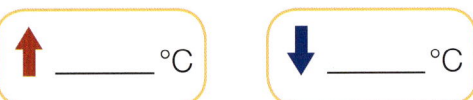

7 What's the difference between the two temperatures? ____________

8 Look at the graphs again and circle the correct answers.

1 The hottest month in Ocho Rios is **August** / **September**.

2 The coldest months in Ocho Rios are **January and February** / **March and April**.

9 Complete the chart with the temperature variation in your city during the week. Then, create a bar graph to represent it.

Day of the week	Min °C	Max °C
Sunday		
Monday		
Tuesday		
Wednesday		
Thursday		
Friday		
Saturday		

UNIT 6

CITIES

UNIT 6

HISTORY

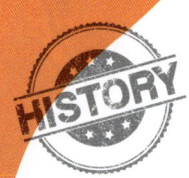

1 Find the words and write them under the pictures.

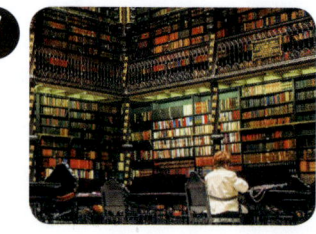

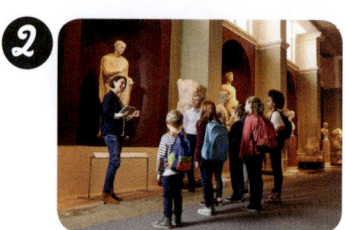

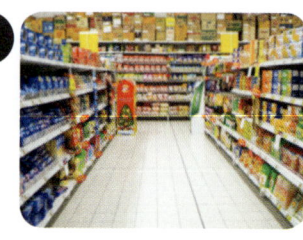

1

____

2

____

3

____

F	S	U	P	E	R	M	A	R	K	E	T
M	O	V	I	E	T	H	E	A	T	E	R
O	H	O	S	P	I	T	A	L	K	R	L
U	H	C	M	U	S	E	U	M	I	X	C
B	K	A	H	T	J	L	W	G	V	M	Q
D	J	F	C	H	Y	L	N	P	T	W	S
S	V	E	Z	Y	A	I	R	P	O	R	T
O	L	I	B	R	A	R	Y	J	R	L	A

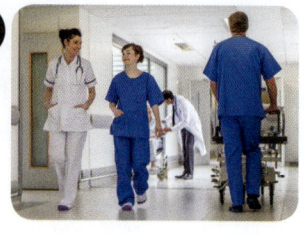

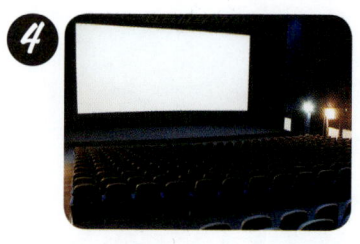

4

____

5

____

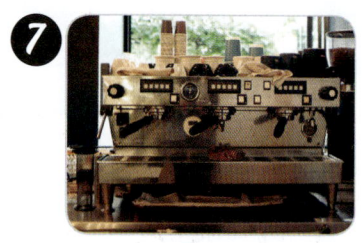

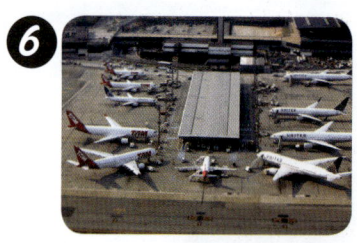

7

____

6

____

2 Which places can you find only in big cities?

____

TRACK 13

3 Listen and read.

First Cities

Where do you think the first cities originated? And when?

Some historians and archaeologists think the first cities emerged in a number of places after the development of **agriculture** and **commerce**. People started cultivating plants and livestock and, having more food, populations started to grow.

But groups of people still lived far from each other and all the food and products needed to be transported long distances. Living together in one place reduced the costs of **transportation**. It also established **political power** over an area.

Some of the first cities originated by the Sumerians in Mesopotamia, around 5400 BCE.

Approximate region of Mesopotamia in a current political map.

Sumerian ruins from 2100 BCE in Iraq.

GLOSSARY

BCE: Before the Common Era

It's a fact!
Mesopotamia means "between rivers" in ancient Greek.

4 Read and complete using the words in **bold** from the text.

1 _____ and _____ promoted the development of cities.

2 When more people started to live together the cost of _____ was reduced.

3 To organize larger groups of people, it was necessary to establish _____.

Think Twice

1 Why do you think the first cities in Mesopotamia emerged near river valleys?

2 What other natural resources or characteristics can help the formation of a city?

TRACK 14

5 Listen and read.

Cities Nowadays

Do you know more people who live in the city or in the country? And around the world, do you think there are more people in rural or in urban areas?

Urbanization is a process in which people migrate from **rural areas** to **cities**. This can happen because they are looking for jobs or more infrastructure.

On one hand, urbanization promotes social and cultural integration and economic development. On the other hand, if the urban growth is not well managed, it can cause inadequate access to water and sanitation, unemployment, pollution, and a lack of housing.

Projections suggest that, by 2050, 68% of the world's population will live in urban areas.

Mumbai, in India, is one of the most densely populated cities.

6 Complete the chart with information from the text.

Urbanization	
positive aspects	negative aspects

Can you think of any other positive or negative aspects?

7 These are sustainable alternatives to some urban problems. Write the problem from Activity 6 they correspond to.

❶ A hotel with vertical gardens.

❷ A social housing project designed for low-income families.

8 In groups, plan a sustainable city. Consider the aspects in the pictures and follow the steps below.

1. Briefly discuss the examples in the pictures.
2. Choose one of the pictures to plan solutions. These pictures are just examples; you can use them or think of other alternatives.
3. Write or draw ideas of solutions for the item you chose.
4. Get together again and decide on a name for your city.
5. Draw the map of your city, showing the solutions you propose.
6. Present your city to the class.

Transport 
Bikes and electric buses

Renewable Energy 
Solar panels

Waste 
Recycling

Food 
Urban farming

Jobs and Economy 
Public job agency

Culture and Leisure 
Art festival

Health 
Preventive activities

RURAL AND URBAN WORK

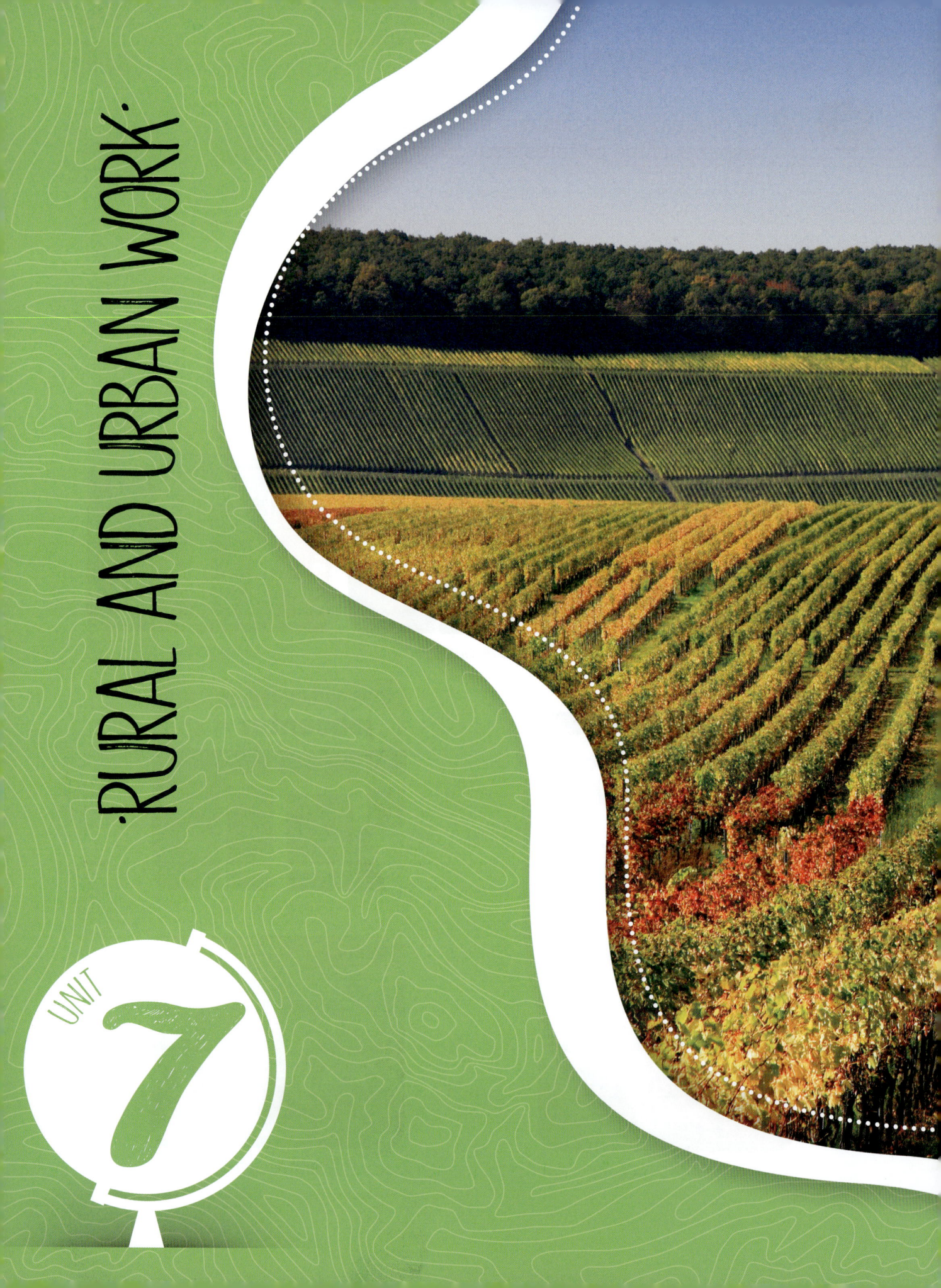

UNIT 7

GEOGRAPHY

This is Bordeaux, a famous wine region in France.

Are there any wine regions in your country?

Look at the picture.

Is this a rural or urban area? Why?

What jobs do you think you can find in this area?

UNIT 7

1. Read the clues and write the name under each picture.

Who's this?

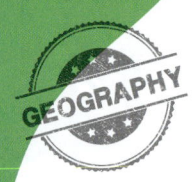

- Matthew cultivates the land and raises animals. He's a **farmer**.
- Joshua takes care of people. He's a **nurse**.
- Tyler takes care of animals. He's a **vet**.
- Kayla catches fish. She's a **fisherwoman**.
- Alex sells products to customers. He's a **clerk**.
- Jessica drives a truck. She's a **truck driver**.
- Harper operates a machine in factory. She's a **factory worker**.
- Amanda rescues people and animals. She's a **firefighter**.

1. Matthew
2. _____
3. _____
4. _____
5. _____
6. _____
7. _____
8. _____

2. Which jobs in Activity 1 are important in the country? Which are important in the city? And in both of them?

_____.

42

TRACK 15

3 Listen and read.

Work in the Country

Most jobs in the country are related to **agriculture**, which is the cultivation of crops and livestock. There is also resource extraction, such as oil, gas, and minerals.

Practices in agriculture

There are two different practices in agriculture. **Subsistence farming** is the production of food that is consumed by the same people who cultivate it. It usually depends on natural methods, with little or no mechanization, pesticides, or fertilizers. **Commercial intensive agriculture** focuses on big consumer markets. It involves large fields and many animals, pesticides and fertilizers, and mechanization.

Generally, in subsistence farming, people cultivate mixed crops in the same area (**polyculture**) and, in commercial intensive agriculture, people cultivate only one crop (**monoculture**), obtaining large harvests with minimal resources.

Changes in agriculture

Some important changes in agriculture include agricultural chemistry (especially in the 20th century), hydroponics, gene manipulation, seed improvement, and others. Since the introduction of agricultural chemistry, now there is also organic farming, with no artificial chemistry.

4 Find and write.

1 What jobs are more common in the country? _____.

2 Which farming is not for commercial purposes? _____.

5 Look at the images and number the words below.

❶ Mass soybean harvest in Brazil.

❷ Vegetable garden in France.

a mechanization ◯   c monoculture ①   e polyculture ◯

b subsistence farm ◯   d intensive agriculture ◯   f pesticides and fertilizers ◯

43

UNIT 7 GEOGRAPHY

TRACK 16

6 Listen and read.

Work in the City

Most industries and businesses are located in cities. Many of the products that come from agriculture and resource extraction are converted into finished products in factories. The number of people who work in factories tends to decrease because technological innovations lead to more automation of the manufacturing process.

After manufacturing, products are sold in stores and supermarkets. In cities, people can work in retail or in many other specific areas. Teachers, for example, work in education. Doctors work in health care; and bus drivers, in transportation. Services provided by the government are called public services. They include health care, electricity, education, infrastructure, and others.

Think Twice

1 Why are there less people working in factories now?

2 What do you think can be done to prevent unemployment?

7 Look at the ad and number. Then write the corresponding sector of the economy.

SEA TO DISH
Eat Fresh Fish

1 Caught by local fishermen.
2 Cleaned and processed.
3 Transported at peak freshness.
4 Sold by your local organic store.
5 Savoured at your own house.

a Retail — 4 — tertiary

b Transporting — ___ — _____

c Fishing — ___ — _____

d Processing — ___ — _____

8 Think about products or services that you and your family use and create an ad for one of them. Follow the steps below.

1 Make a list of three products or services.

- _____
- _____
- _____

2 Choose one product or service of your list. Research about it. Use the following questions to guide you.

> **If it's a product**
> - Where does it come from? _____.
> - What type of factory transforms it into a finished product? Describe the process.
>   _____.
> - How is it transported and distributed?
>   _____.
> - Where can you buy this product?
>   _____.

> **If it's a service**
> - What professional offers it? _____.
> - What does this professional need to study in order to do it?
>   _____.
> - What certificates does this professional need to have?
>   _____.
> - Where can you find this service?
>   _____.

3 Create your ad. Show the steps of production or the qualities of the professionals involved. Look back at Activity 7 for inspiration.

4 Hang your ad on the classroom wall and walk around to check your classmates' ads. Did you find another ad for your product or service?

CALENDARS

UNIT 8

SCIENCE

This is the Earth, our planet. It turns around its axis once every 24 hours approximately.

What's the name of the star behind the Earth in this picture?

Look at the picture.

The side you see in the picture is not illuminated by the Sun. Is it daytime or nighttime there?

If it's night in Japan, what time of day is it in the USA? Why?

UNIT 8 — SCIENCE

1 Complete the calendar with the names of the months.

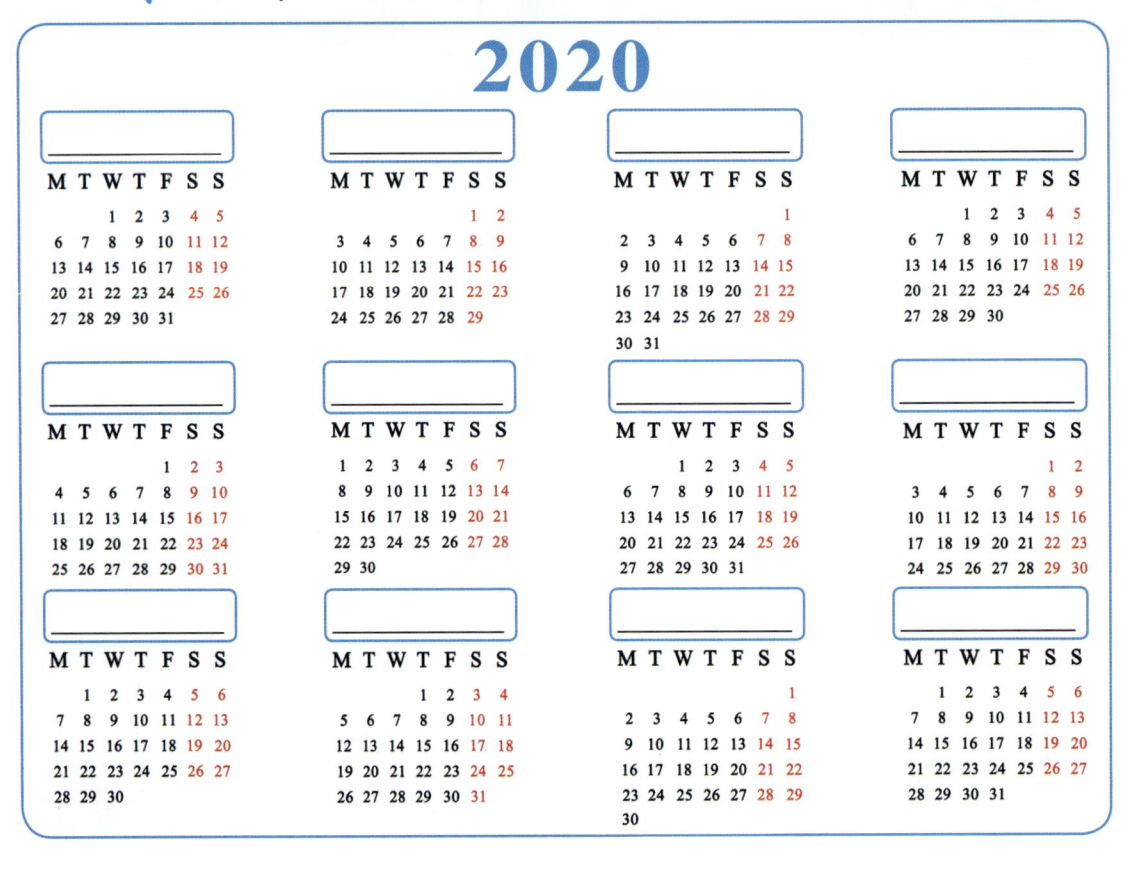

2020

_____	_____	_____	_____
M T W T F S S	M T W T F S S	M T W T F S S	M T W T F S S
1 2 3 4 5	1 2	1	1 2 3 4 5
6 7 8 9 10 11 12	3 4 5 6 7 8 9	2 3 4 5 6 7 8	6 7 8 9 10 11 12
13 14 15 16 17 18 19	10 11 12 13 14 15 16	9 10 11 12 13 14 15	13 14 15 16 17 18 19
20 21 22 23 24 25 26	17 18 19 20 21 22 23	16 17 18 19 20 21 22	20 21 22 23 24 25 26
27 28 29 30 31	24 25 26 27 28 29	23 24 25 26 27 28 29	27 28 29 30
		30 31	
_____	_____	_____	_____
M T W T F S S	M T W T F S S	M T W T F S S	M T W T F S S
1 2 3	1 2 3 4 5 6 7	1 2 3 4 5	1 2
4 5 6 7 8 9 10	8 9 10 11 12 13 14	6 7 8 9 10 11 12	3 4 5 6 7 8 9
11 12 13 14 15 16 17	15 16 17 18 19 20 21	13 14 15 16 17 18 19	10 11 12 13 14 15 16
18 19 20 21 22 23 24	22 23 24 25 26 27 28	20 21 22 23 24 25 26	17 18 19 20 21 22 23
25 26 27 28 29 30 31	29 30	27 28 29 30 31	24 25 26 27 28 29 30
_____	_____	_____	_____
M T W T F S S	M T W T F S S	M T W T F S S	M T W T F S S
1 2 3 4 5 6	1 2 3 4	1	1 2 3 4 5 6
7 8 9 10 11 12 13	5 6 7 8 9 10 11	2 3 4 5 6 7 8	7 8 9 10 11 12 13
14 15 16 17 18 19 20	12 13 14 15 16 17 18	9 10 11 12 13 14 15	14 15 16 17 18 19 20
21 22 23 24 25 26 27	19 20 21 22 23 24 25	16 17 18 19 20 21 22	21 22 23 24 25 26 27
28 29 30	26 27 28 29 30 31	23 24 25 26 27 28 29	28 29 30 31
		30	

2 Look at the month of July and answer the questions.

1 What day does July begin on? _____.

2 What day will July finish on? _____.

3 How many Saturdays are there in July? _____.

3 Look at the calendar and write the number of days next to each month.

January __31__   February _____   March _____   April _____

May _____   June _____   July _____   August _____

September _____   October _____   November _____   December _____

> Can you see any pattern?
> _____.

48

TRACK 17

4 Listen and read.

Astronomical Cycles

Astronomy is the study of celestial objects such as stars, planets, and comets. Throughout history, people have used natural astronomical time intervals to help measure the passage of time.

The main astronomical cycles are the **day**, the **month**, and the **year**. The day is based on the rotation of the Earth on its axis, which takes approximately 24 hours. The month is based on the revolution of the moon around the Earth, which is around 27 days, and the year is based on the revolution of the Earth around the Sun, which lasts 365 days.

Earth's Revolution and Rotation

revolution

rotation

The Earth takes a day to rotate around its axis and a year to revolve around the Sun.

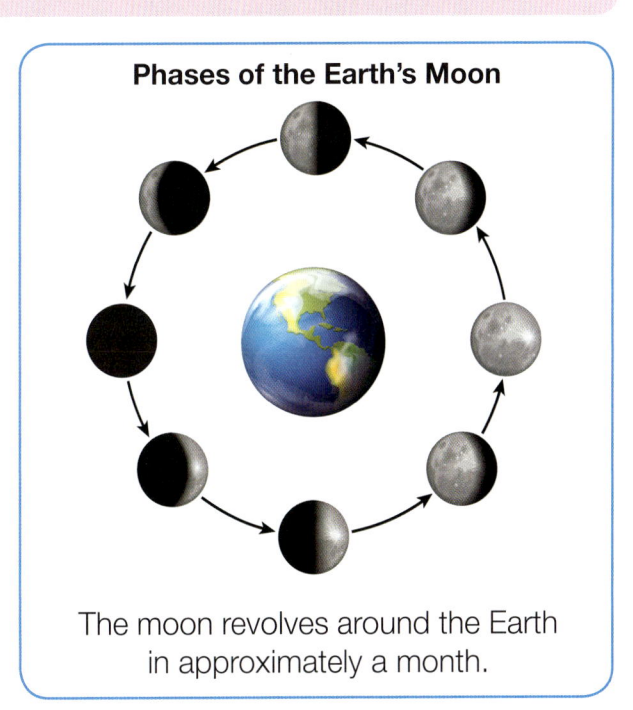

Phases of the Earth's Moon

The moon revolves around the Earth in approximately a month.

5 Read and write.

1 What is astronomy?

2 What is the relationship between astronomy and calendars?

6 Match.

day	revolution of the Earth around the Sun	27 days
month	rotation of the Earth on its axis	24 hours
year	revolution of the moon around the Earth	365 days

49

TRACK 18

7 Listen and read.

Early Calendars

Ancient cultures also needed to keep track of time. In order to plan the agricultural cycle, like planting and harvesting, it is essential to understand the seasons and have a calendar.

The Stonehenge, for example, in the UK, was used to monitor the motions of the Sun and the moon.

Stonehenge is located in England.

The Gregorian Calendar

The calendar used nowadays in most countries of the world is called the Gregorian calendar. It is named after Pope Gregory XIII, who introduced it. It consists of a year with 12 months, each month with 28 to 31 days. The date is specified by the month, day, and year. For example, January 22, 2019.

Pope Gregory XIII

8 Read and answer.

1 What is the name of the calendar most people use nowadays?
_____.

2 Do you know of any other calendars used in the world? Which ones?
_____
_____.

9 Do some research on the calendars below.

Aztec calendar	traditional Chinese calendar
Basic characteristics: _____ _____ _____	Basic characteristics: _____ _____ _____

10 Choose one of the calendars above and follow these steps.

   1 Do some more research and choose an element to represent graphically.

   2 Draw it or make a collage by printing, pasting, and coloring.

   3 Plan a small presentation for your classmates:

   - Let them first guess what you have represented.
   - Explain what it is and why you chose it.

LET'S CELEBRATE!

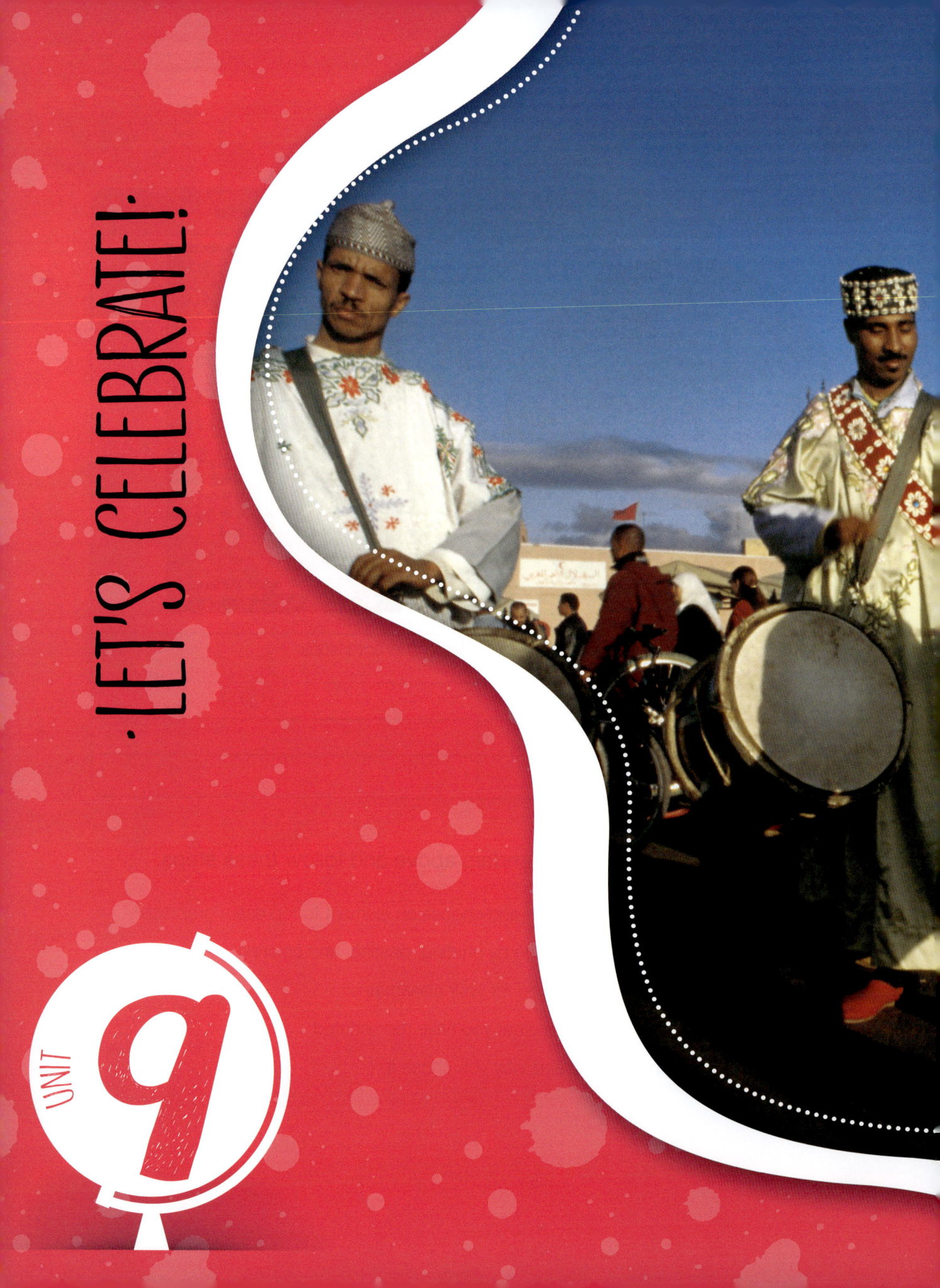

UNIT 9

ART

This picture shows musicians performing at Gnaoua World Music Festival, in Morocco.

Do you go to festivals in your country? Which ones?

Look at the picture.
What time of day do you think this is?

ZOOM IN

Can you name any instrument that they are playing?

UNIT 9

ART

1 Match the pictures to the corresponding words. Then answer.

barbecue   birthday party   parade   picnic   wedding

1. _____
2. _____
3. _____
4. _____
5. _____

Are any of these events popular in your country? Which ones?
_____.

TRACK 19

2 Listen and read.

Traditional Celebrations

Traditional celebrations are connected to the overall cultural identity of a country or community. Weddings, harvest festivals, and religious holidays are some examples.

In these events, we can see or be part of many forms of artistic expressions. For example, we can dance and sing if we take part in a Carnival parade in Brazil. We can play the spoons as a kind of percussion to follow Irish musicians in a traditional festival. We can cover our whole body in bright colors at the Holi festival in India.

Celebrating your traditions helps keep you grounded in your own culture.

3 Read and answer.

1 Why are traditional celebrations important?

_____

2 What are some examples of celebrations?

_____

TRACK 20

4 Listen and read.

Albuquerque International Balloon Fiesta
Place: Albuquerque, New Mexico, USA.
Kids and adults gather to launch balloons of all shapes, colors, and sizes.

Yi Peng Lantern Festival
Place: Chiang Mai, Thailand.
Thousands of lanterns are released in the sky to wish for good fortune in the new year. This happens on the evening of the full moon on the 12th month of the Thai Lunar calendar.

Unit 9

La Tomatina
Place: Buñol, Spain.

Starting in 1945, the tomato-throwing festival happens every year. Some people say the tradition began with a food fight among friends.

Carnival
Place: Rio de Janeiro, Brazil.

Rio's Carnival is the largest carnival in the world. For five days, there are lots of music, dance, and costumes on the streets and in the Sambodromo, a stadium built for the festival. Samba schools parade their colorful costumes and huge floats to the rhythm of original samba songs.

Harbin International Ice and Snow Sculpture Festival
Place: Harbin, Heilongjiang, China.

It is the biggest snow festival in the world. Huge ice sculptures are built for the festival that began in 1963.

5 Read and answer.

1 Where does Rio's Carnival take place?

_____

_____.

2 When does the Yi Peng Lantern Festival happen?

_____

_____.

3 What is the name of the biggest snow festival in the world?

_____

_____.

4 Is La Tomatina a religious festival?

_____

_____.

5 What do people launch in the air in Albuquerque, USA?

_____

_____.

6 Which festival called your attention the most? Why?

_____

_____.

6 In groups, research about a traditional festival in your country. Complete the chart.

place	
time of year	
historical background	
people involved	
number of visitors	

7 Share your research with your classmates. You can draw and explain it to them or you can act out a relevant part of the festival.

MATTER AND CHANGES

UNIT 10

SCIENCE

When liquid water turns into gas, we call this process *evaporation*. When can you see water evaporating?

Look at the picture. Why does the water evaporate?

UNIT 10

SCIENCE

1 Write the materials' names and what they are made of.

| ~~clothes~~ ~~fabric~~ furniture glass plastic toys windows wood |

1

_____Clothes_____ are made of _____fabric_____.

2

_____ can be made of _____.

3

_____ can be made of _____.

4

_____ are made of _____.

> Materials have different properties. For example, fabric is soft and wood is hard.

2 Write the names of some objects made out of these materials.

plastic	fabric	wood	glass

60

TRACK 21

3 Listen and read.

What Is Matter?

Everything around you is matter: plants, animals, air, objects, food, water, etc.

Matter is anything that has **mass** and **occupies space** (it has **volume**). All matter is made up of particles that are called atoms. Material properties, for example, depend on the kinds of atom the material is made from.

States of matter

Matter is found in three states: solid, liquid, and gas. A **solid** has a definite shape. A **liquid** flows and does not have a definite shape. Most **gases** are invisible and can flow.

Solid
(particles so close they form a solid bond)

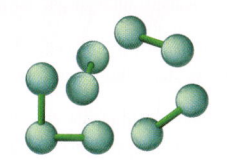

Liquid
(particles close together)

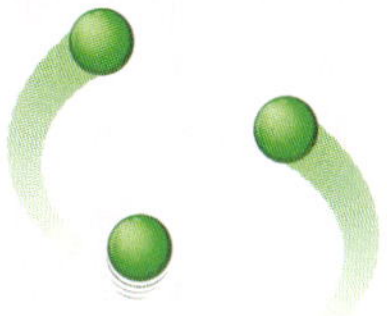

Gas
(particles far apart)

GLOSSARY

Mass: The amount of matter in an object.
Volume: The amount of space something occupies.

Think Twice

1 Why do solids have a definite shape?
2 And why don't liquids and gases?

4 Write *solid*, *liquid*, or *gas*.

_____   _____   _____

TRACK 22

5 Listen and read.

Physical Changes

Matter can move from one state to another if heated or cooled. When a substance changes from a liquid to a gas, for example, this is called a **physical change**. In a physical change, the substance is the same and it is usually easy to reverse the change.

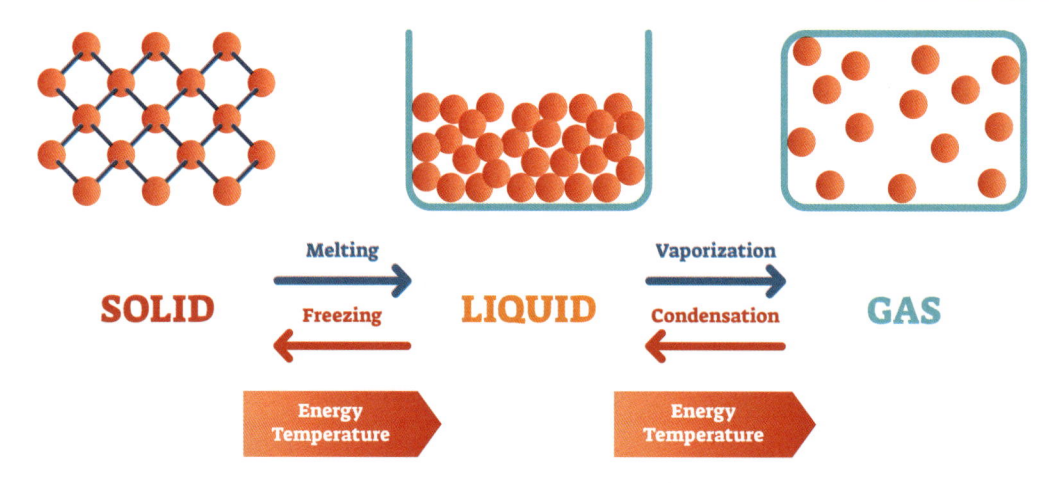

Melting ice cream is a physical change.

SOLID — Melting → / ← Freezing — LIQUID — Vaporization → / ← Condensation — GAS

Energy Temperature

Energy Temperature

Chemical Changes

In chemical changes, a new substance is created. This kind of change can produce gases, a change in color, temperature, taste, or texture. Since a new substance is formed, most chemical changes cannot be reversed.

A cooked egg suffered a chemical change.

6 Read and write.

1 What is the difference between a physical and a chemical change?
2 Can a physical change be reversed? And a chemical one?

7 Write *physical* or *chemical* (change) according to the situation.

1 fermentation _____
2 boiling water _____
3 breaking glass _____
4 burning wood _____

8 Let's make blueberry muffins! Work with your teacher and classmates.

Blueberry Muffins

1 1/2 cups flour

2 teaspoons baking powder

1 cup fresh blueberries

1/4 teaspoon salt

1 egg

3/4 cup white sugar plus 1 tablespoon for muffin tops

1/3 cup milk

1/3 cup vegetable oil

Directions

Preheat oven to 200 °C.
Combine the flour, sugar, salt, and baking powder.
Place vegetable oil into one cup. Add the egg and enough milk to fill the cup.
Mix this with the flour mixture and add the blueberries.
Grease muffin cups and fill them with the dough.
Add a small sprinkle of sugar on top.
Bake until the muffins are risen and lightly brown on top (20-30 minutes in the preheated oven).

9 Read and write.

1 Is this a physical or chemical change? Why?

_____.

2 Why do we need to put the muffin in the oven?

_____.

2020 © Macmillan Education do Brasil

Director of Languages Brazil: Patrícia Souza De Luccia
Publishing Manager and Field Researcher: Patricia Muradas
Content Creation Coordinator: Cristina do Vale
Art Editor: Jean Aranha
Content Development: Ana Elisa Martins
Content Editors: Ana Beatriz da Costa Moreira, Daniela Gonçala da Costa, Luciana Pereira da Silva
Digital Editor: Ana Paula Girardi
Editorial Assistant: Roberta Somera
Editorial Intern: Bruna Marques
Art Assistant: Denis Araujo
Art Intern: Jacqueline Alves
Graphic Production: Tatiane Romano, Thais Mendes P. Galvão
Proofreaders: Edward Willson, Márcia Leme, Sabrina Cairo Bileski
Design Concept: Design Divertido Artes Gráficas
Page Make-Up: Figurattiva Editorial
Photo Research: Marcia Sato
Image Processing: Jean Aranha, Jacqueline Alves, Denis Araujo
Audio: Argila Music, Núcleo de Criação
Cover Concept: Jean Aranha
Cover photography: FrankyDeMeyer/iStockphoto/Getty Images, Bubert/iStockphoto/Getty Images, LokFung/iStockphoto/Getty Images, Photoco/iStockphoto/Getty Images
Illustrations: Gustavo Gialuca (p. 15, 30, 31, 49, 61, 62, 63).

Reproduction prohibited. Penal Code Article 184 and Law number 9.610 of February 19, 1998.

We would like to dedicate this book to teachers all over Brazil. We would also like to thank our clients and teachers who have helped us make this book better with their many rich contributions and feedback straight from the classroom!

The authors and publishers would like to thank the following for permission to reproduce the photographic material:

p. 4: abalcazar/iStockphoto/Getty Images; p. 6: lamyai/iStockphoto/Getty Images, idealistock/iStockphoto/Getty Images, baona/iStockphoto/Getty Images, BLFink/iStockphoto/Getty Images, Tryaging/iStockphoto/Getty Images, Santje09/iStockphoto/Getty Images, ugurhan/iStockphoto/Getty Images, Tramino/iStockphoto/Getty Images; p. 7: Maxiphoto/iStockphoto/Getty Images, Marat Musabirov/iStockphoto/Getty Images, pidjoe/iStockphoto/Getty Images, Roman_Baiadin/iStockphoto/Getty Images, Tarzhanova/iStockphoto/Getty Images, yorkfoto/iStockphoto/Getty Images; p. 8: Dimitrios Karamitros/iStockphoto/Getty Images, ibrahimusta/iStockphoto/Getty Images, JaCZhou/iStockphoto/Getty Images; p. 10-11: monkeybusinessimages/iStockphoto/Getty Images; p. 12: acceptfoto/iStockphoto/Getty Images, juefraphoto/iStockphoto/Getty Images; p. 13: pixelfit/iStockphoto/Getty Images, monticelllo/iStockphoto/Getty Images, ollo/iStockphoto/Getty Images, zorandimzr/iStockphoto/Getty Images, tudiocasper/iStockphoto/Getty Images, hidesy/iStockphoto/Getty Images, Volosina/iStockphoto/Getty Images, studiocasper/iStockphoto/Getty Images; p. 14: danishkhan/iStockphoto/Getty Images, Traimak_Ivan/iStockphoto/Getty Images, andresr/iStockphoto/Getty Images; p. 15: FG Trade/iStockphoto/Getty Images, FatCamera/iStockphoto/Getty Images, mangostock/iStockphoto/Getty Images, Kharlamova/iStockphoto/Getty Images; p. 16: stacey_newman/iStockphoto/Getty Images; p. 18: Poligrafistka/iStockphoto/Getty Images, tinnakorn/iStockphoto/Getty Images, Leontura/iStockphoto/Getty Images, liangpv/iStockphoto/Getty Images, Poligrafistka/iStockphoto/Getty Images, liangpv/iStockphoto/Getty Images, Poligrafistka/iStockphoto/Getty Images, Graphic_photo/iStockphoto/Getty Images; p. 19: Glow Images; p. 20: Alamy/Fotoarena, Joel Carillet/iStockphoto/Getty Images, johncopland/iStockphoto/Getty Images; p. 21: monkeybusinessimages/iStockphoto/Getty Images, Pulsar Imagens; p. 22: Daisy-Daisy/iStockphoto/Getty Images; p. 24: MajaMitrovic/iStockphoto/Getty Images, MajaMitrovic/iStockphoto/Getty Images, wsantina/iStockphoto/Getty Images, Ismailciydem/iStockphoto/Getty Images, Darunechka/iStockphoto/Getty Images, garymilner/iStockphoto/Getty Images; p. 25: vm/iStockphoto/Getty Images, PeopleImages/iStockphoto/Getty Images; p. 26: Sidekick/iStockphoto/Getty Images, Dmytro Aksonov/iStockphoto/Getty Images, RBFried/iStockphoto/Getty Images, ChristopherBernard/iStockphoto/Getty Images, isitsharp/iStockphoto/Getty Images, monkeybusinessimages/iStockphoto/Getty Images; p. 27: DmitriyKazitsyn/iStockphoto/Getty Images, dejan Jekic/iStockphoto/Getty Images, somchaisom/iStockphoto/Getty Images; p. 28: wdstock/iStockphoto/Getty Images; p. 30: Sashkinw/iStockphoto/Getty Images; p. 31: TheArtist/iStockphoto/Getty Images, oleksii arseniuk/iStockphoto/Getty Images, Bohdanochka/iStockphoto/Getty Images; p. 34: tifonimages/iStockphoto/Getty Images; p. 36: Alex Jenkins/iStockphoto/Getty Images, monkeybusinessimages/iStockphoto/Getty Images, AEKKARAT DOUNGMANEERATTANA/iStockphoto/Getty Images, perets/iStockphoto/Getty Images, Spotmatik/iStockphoto/Getty Images, upungato/iStockphoto/Getty Images, baranozdemir/iStockphoto/Getty Images; p. 37: HomoCosmicos/iStockphoto/Getty Images, meshaphoto/iStockphoto/Getty Images; p. 38: aluxum/iStockphoto/Getty Images; p. 39: minemero/iStockphoto/Getty Images, WangAnQi/iStockphoto/Getty Images, Kanawa_Studio/iStockphoto/Getty Images, BrasilNut1/iStockphoto/Getty Images, AP Photo/Getty Images, wjarek/iStockphoto/Getty Images, PaulMcKinnon/iStockphoto/Getty Images; p. 40: AVTG/iStockphoto/Getty Images; p. 42: Andree_Nery/iStockphoto/Getty Images, kali9/iStockphoto/Getty Images, andresr/iStockphoto/Getty Images, shironosov/iStockphoto/Getty Images, sturti/iStockphoto/Getty Images, Scoth Dickerson/Easypix, martin-dm/iStockphoto/Getty Images, Antonio_Diaz/iStockphoto/Getty Images; p. 44: Radist/iStockphoto/Getty Images; p. 46: I love takeing photos/iStockphoto/Getty Images; p. 48: SyhinStas/iStockphoto/Getty Images, Dimitris66/iStockphoto/Getty Images; p. 49: b44022101/iStockphoto/Getty Images, blueringmedia/iStockphoto/Getty Images; p. 50: MajaPhoto/iStockphoto/Getty Images, Coleção privada; p. 51: RapidEye/iStockphoto/Getty Images, HansJoachim/iStockphoto/Getty Images; p. 52: Remanz/iStockphoto/Getty Images; p. 54: FG Trade/iStockphoto/Getty Images, rvimages/iStockphoto/Getty Images, FatCamera/iStockphoto/Getty Images, nd3000/iStockphoto/Getty Images, stu99/iStockphoto/Getty Images; p. 55: duckycards/iStockphoto/Getty Images, sihasakprachum/iStockphoto/Getty Images; p. 56: Alberto Saiz/AP Photo/Getty Images, FernandoQuevedo/iStockphoto/Getty Images, LeonU/iStockphoto/Getty Images; p. 57: Global_Pics/iStockphoto/Getty Images, pedrorufo/iStockphoto/Getty Images; p. 58: JasonDoiy/iStockphoto/Getty Images; p. 60: bonetta/iStockphoto/Getty Images, skodonnell/iStockphoto/Getty Images, John_Kasawa/iStockphoto/Getty Images, antikainen/iStockphoto/Getty Images; p. 61: ttsz/iStockphoto/Getty Images.

Dados Internacionais de Catalogação na Publicação (CIP)
Bibliotecária responsável: Aline Graziele Benitez CRB-1/3129

M294n Martins, Ana Elisa Teixeira
1.ed.   Next Station CLIL Book 3 / Ana Elisa Teixeira Martins. – 1.ed. – São Paulo: Macmillan Education do Brasil, 2020.
64 p.; il.; 21 x 27 cm. – (Coleção Next Station)
ISBN: 978-85-511-0149-0 (aluno)
978-85-511-0154-4 (professor)
1. Língua inglesa. I. Título.

Índice para catálogo sistemático:

1. Língua inglesa

All rights reserved.

MACMILLAN EDUCATION DO BRASIL
Av. Brigadeiro Faria Lima, 1.309, 3º Andar – Jd. Paulistano – São Paulo – SP – 01452-002
www.macmillan.com.br
Customer Service: [55] (11) 4613-2278
0800 16 88 77
Fax: [55] (11) 4612-6098

Printed in Brazil. First print. July, 2019.